Night of the Hawk

Night
of the
Hawk

poems

Lauren Martin

SHE WRITES PRESS

Published 2024
Printed in the United States of America
Print ISBN: 978-1-64742-658-3
E-ISBN: 978-1-64742-659-0
Library of Congress Control Number: [LOCCN]

For information, address:
She Writes Press
1569 Solano Ave #546
Berkeley, CA 94707

Interior design by Stacey Aaronson

She Writes Press is a division of SparkPoint Studio, LLC.

For the Chibok girls and all other girls living in captivity and abuse. May freedom be yours.

TABLE OF CONTENTS

POETRY KEY

Ifá – Yorùbá religion. Ifá is considered the word of almighty God or the true oracle. Ifá is also what someone has when they are initiated to the religion.

Olódùmarè – God in Yorùbá

Òrìsà – are manifestations of God that are worshipped and propitiated as a means of communicating with Olódùmarè. Many were essential elementals that came from heaven, others were human beings who, when they ascended, became elementals.

Òsun – one of the Òrìsà in the Yorùbá pantheon, Òsun is the Goddess of the river, also the maternal figure in Ifá, and was essential in the creation of all existence when God/Olódùmarè sent elemental Gods from heaven to create earth.

Esù – the intermediary between the two realms (heaven and earth/ or Òrìsà to Òrìsà) who manages interference or blessings.

Ìyàmi – the great mothers, primordial femininity; witches, essential to the spirit realm.

Ògún – was a warrior who ascended, and is now the God of iron and steel.

Yemoja – called the mother of fishes. The Òrìsà that governs oceans and waters.

Sàngó – the Òrìsà of thunder and lightning, married to and working with Oya.

Oya – the Òrìsà of the wind, death and change; essential to the manifestation and tempering of Sàngó.

Egbé – astral spirits

Irúnmolè – all the Òrìsà

Odù – UNESCO named the Ifá divination system as a masterpiece of the intangible cultural heritage of humanity. Within the Ifá religion, casting of the sacred oracle is essential. Each of the sacred oral texts is classified as an Odù and when people are initiated to the religion, each person receives an Odù in the process of initiation that applies to them and their destiny.

Igbódù – the sacred grove used for initiation

Àse – prayer; similar to amen; spiritual energy

Haúsá – there are three major tribes in Nigeria: Haúsá, Ígbò, Yorùbá. The Chibok girls are mostly Haúsá.

ESSENTIALS OF MAN

Give me peace
Give me hope
Give me a soul
From which to stand

OSCEOLA

I dream
Of Africa
When I wake
And watch the sun
Refract beyond the large
Schoolyard Oak
Sitting West
Where the Ravens nest
And the Hawks seek their young
I dream of a strong woman
And solitude
The sounds of nature
Giving way to perspective
Nobility of spirit
Being recognized
By a strong man
Wanting debates
And nights of passion
As unafraid
Of female intellect
And post menopausal
Sensuality as
A great hunt

AS THE BOW BREAKS

As the bow breaks
I refuse to be broken
I have been beaten
Many times by men

By eleven
I knew it well
The feeling of steeling myself
Against the lies of others

Some fire of dignity
That has always lived within me
Far from the stretches of fear
Finally outpaced and trapped
you go small
as embers burn

Rage ignites
At the unfairness of that control
For I am not confused
I am able to accept being this clear
In the face of your confusion about me
Forced by survival to be silent

My certainty will haunt you
In whatever intuitive way you identify
When I have not relented
to your insecurity
and distortion
You want to beat me harder
But my knowledge will only deepen

NIGHT OF THE HAWK

Night of the black hawk
And the still bird
And the silvery moon

You Ìyàmi keep
Calling to me

When I have wandered
long enough
what am I still beholden to?
I have told you
All things
frozen
in time
Around us

I will give you what you want
In measure
In reason

There are obligations
I know this
My Odù

For it is you that lives
In the Igbódù
It is you that lives
In the grave
and
In the souls of men
Possessed with greed

It is you that lives
To bring the bounty
To chase away death
To shower with crimson and gold
The recipient
Waiting for so long

Amber is the eye
That sees through the night
And chooses
Carefully picking prey
Or friend
Or foe

Appeased as you must be
Restored to your honor
Intermingled with your existence
Is the realm of life
and
Generosity

MY EXPERIENCE AS A POSTMENOPAUSAL WOMAN

Is we are ignored
        Everywhere – even in poetry

Somehow not romantic or feminist
enough
Our wisdom excluded as undignified
As undignified as women running into the cold night with hot
flashes peeling layers

"We're not helping men into the
conversation by making them feel
emasculated"   I say

And experience a new version of "blame the victim."

One in which there is no respect for the
elder authority of the endocrine system
and years of misogyny with no
conversation. Where we screamed into
the Grand Canyon that blew dust back
into our faces on the hot wind

I am told that I lack some insight that is
honored and reflected in youth   rather
        must reflect my inability as an
"old feminist" to differentiate between my
"internalized misogyny" and what is
unbalanced

To be told that you have no idea when
We paved the way
When I am standing on the shoulders
of my own mother

You don't see me

And maybe that's because you're
Not looking down
To the foundation of   my shoulders
To the years of my sleeves rolled up
And boots tied high
At rallies and secret activist meetings
Countless abuses of power
Soul changing assaults

I can see the context of our culture
Then and now
And am happy you are bashing
The door open
Breaking the
Glass ceiling
But it's not because   we didn't try
Of course we did
Our height lets you touch
                                        the glass with
your hammer

PEACHES

Dear Peaches,

Please stop killing yourself with shameful behavior. I saw the ass drums. I wanted to barf. I thought much more highly of you. You are the slimy lecherous guy on stage at spring break. Except you're 60. I guess that makes sense. But what is going on? And you question my rituals?
Love,
Muñequita

SPIROCHETE

Oh Lyme Disease
You bitch

This morning you
Split my lip
Why?
Because you could

And now I look
Like I was punched
– In the face, no less –
Every smile hurts

Daily, monthly
You rob me
Like an addict cousin
Who hits me
Over the head with
My own purse

Now the IRS
Denies expenses
For a disease the
Government says
Doesn't exist

I'm working
I'm trying
I haven't given up
Please, you filthy biofilm
Stop

ÒSUN WÈ MÍMÓ

Òsun, Òsun
I ask you
To wash me clean
Clean of the stained
And bridled nature
That has been my life

Those that know you
Know the gentleness
With which you speak
But in seemingly
Trivial matters

Like all women after you
Your message is clear
Often unheard
Until dams burst
And tears flood
The horizon

I am the river
The river of waters
That funnels food
Of potentiation

Of work once dry
In drought
Of fields of exclusion
Needing Àse

You bring yourself
To all things

And I call you
Now
To be
Adorned

AS THE BOW BREAKS, PART TWO

Dew in the air
On the porch
I bounced
I was walking
Deep into the unsafe night
Of the Bywater
Without money, my things

You forced me back
Put your hands on me
Blocked the exit of the porch
Demanded eye contact

That must be the worst assault to integrity
Forcing someone into your sphere
With separation
No longer a choice

Moisture and sounds surround me
Night. The train. Your drunk voice.
Your wife. Sewing.
She sewed so stilly
A soft light and a drink beside her
It was almost beautiful

I could hear her sympathy
Her gratitude that it was me
Not her
Fear that coiled her into
This life
Convincing her slowly she was free.

I am free. You do not have me
And you never will.
You are antsy and dwarfed
By my determination
And you have broken this friendship
Forever

FOR MOTHS OF UNFORESEEN CAUSAL EVENTS

I poured libations this morning
and caught a moth
Hiding in Èsù's cup
Scrambling in the gin
I thought about how many men
Are plucked up suddenly by God
Into the chaos of decisions not their own
War. Loss. Armament. Outsourcing. Downsizing. Persecution.
Left floundering
For the safety of that dawn comfort
And perceptible obscurity
Hidden in the edge of a hanging cup
Barriers to a life
That somehow we think is
Guaranteed.

IMPACT

i.
I've often wondered
When in core pain
Venturing into public spaces
How many others are feeling like me?
Bursting at the seams with pain and panic.
Do they also worry they might jump up and scream?
Or slide down their seats into the fetal position?
We all get that measure is illusion and pretense
And yet, if eruptions happen, we scowl in judgment.

ii.
people always ask
about forgiveness

or how to glean the good from
total betrayal

why can't virtue be stolen
and undermined

isn't that the unpredictable
nature of things

why can't violation be a responsibility
that people bear

forming a life
in circumstance

as glaciers carved
mountains

FRANKY

sometimes I feel hunted
by my own dog

she stares through me
piercing the horror

of some supposed neglect
I cannot find

some great burden in her
suggests complex emotion

from the bowery
to park place

she has adjusted fine
and seems utterly

intent on eating
most of the time

I began to wonder
if I should play dead

ignore her
as she ignores restriction

but became certain
she would consider me an option

THE WAITING TREE

In Nigeria
Time is specific
Dawn is 6am
Dusk is 6pm

When time
Rises
Distinct sounds
And smells

Afford the knowledge
Of day
The lady next door
Lighting her fire

Backing her child
The scuffling
Of goats
Beginning to graze

The rooster call
The movement of
Family
To scrape teeth

In the dawn
Foggy light
With chewing sticks
Bright white and strong

I can see out
Over layers of
High trees
And small villages

The distance
Of that image carries
On forever
Like a mirage

White birds
Fly upriver
Landing on the
Big tree, synchronistic

They wait there all day
And then life feels
Secure
Knowing they are planted

Forming a border
Until dusk
When they begin
To travel back

Down river
To wherever it is
They sleep
Remain as a unit

I keep thinking
About the girls
Girls taken from
The tree of school

Where they were safely
Planted
In their
Daylight home

How they never
Flew back
Down river
To the waiting

The waiting tree
Of limbs
Of their Haúsá
Mothers and fathers

Pulling them back
Into the folds of protection
Where they belong
In darkness

Darkness
Which in Nigeria
Is completely blanketed
But still alive with noise

As power
Lives in Ghana
Or a generator
But is still billed for

These daughters
So close
Known to the parents
In their location

Parents who were
Asked to wait
Wait for the authorities
To move

While outrage
And public
Insistence
Slipped into stream

Funneling away
Over Òsun
Stones
Leaving

Mother's hearts
Broken
Fathers
Helpless to

Protect them
Or return them
Living in
Stasis

While young
Girls become
Young women
Or gone

And parents
Must wonder
Do I go to spare
The guilt of inactivity

Knowing death
Will eliminate
Saving
And incur loss?

Wretched is
Such a choice
When deprivation
And confusion combine

Giving no
Standard happenings
Watched for
Or familiar

Not the woman
Or her stove
Not the green tree
With the white birds

Just the hollow
Sound
Of space
Where once there was routine

YEMOJA SPEAKS TO SCOTT PRUITT

Oh fish tonight
The child of joy is here
He who seizes the world
And the eldership of flight

Why young brother
Would you poison your mother?
Lifting sin upon sin

They clean my shores
A riddance of the other day
That comes for future 1000 ways

Guardian of souls
Olódùmarè sent here
With chicken scratch

To create my coast
And now in this essential hour
You forgot my epic power

Oh heat me and fill me
I rise above lines
As you distract all those

Within the mines
Oh worker among worker
One son once knew

The power from which
My children grew
I am humble enough

To beg once more
For all must respect
The ocean floor

There is enough,
You have taken enough!

Please calm your inner turmoil

And leave me be before I boil
My brink upon your coin clink

Oh tempest watch as Oya comes
Bringing Sàngó force

A banishment!

Will preserve our days again
When simple children
Cause the end.

OVER THE DAY

Over the day
Around the sun
And I know my home
Wasn't a functional one

Round the clock
And away with time
For I know the years
Have been unkind

Find the chase
And free the spree
Thus bring my love
Back to me

In the house
At half past three
Or shadow will get
The best of ye

CSF

I can't turn left
I can't turn right
I lay here
like a mummy
in a tempurpedic sarcophagus

it has been months
a year
years
my life has passed
in a bed spin
a purgatory

every day
I have ridden the rough seas
of my bedroom
where the walls
mock me

like a funhouse
in the making
I feel suffocated
by the lack of choice
and reach out

for options
and hope
obsessively searching
for signs of improvement
and faith

1969

I'm starting to forget my age
Leave sheets of paper unfound

The documents of
My time here

When I was a child
I wanted to age

As a child of 28
I scoffed at vanity

And now I look on
And want not to remember

Beyond the arrogance
Of easy smiles

Of eyes
Not yet crepey

The reminder of hopes
Dashed

Paths dissected
By destiny

I can see how
Befuddlement and

Forgetting
Becomes a friend

AS THE BOW BREAKS, PART THREE

You are my father.
My father.
To forge your child in rejection

Maybe there are things that remain undone
Tattered in the wind

And yet
I arrive for moments
After insistence of not

Still searching
For something
So essential.

Do I expect that
Of my mother?
Or once you

Inhabit the womb
You know
Love –

Sense the deep
Inner parts
Of your mother's

Essence
Will always
Reach out for you.

But your father
My
Father

Has needs
For himself
And private

Acknowledgment
And pride
Unknown

To me
Recounted by
Others

Giving me
A voyeur's
Glimpse

Into
Some heart
And admiration.

BOOZE

there was a time
when i was drinking in
bottles and bodies
lost amongst them
through pain and diversion
i never knew

that thirty years would pass
and it would still sit so close
  that impulse to be wild and raw and say fuck it

i love that part of myself
as much as i hate it
so alive and vibrant
until i roll on the floor
with shame and humiliation
where where where
  was my limit
  my demarcation point of control that i never found
i had to retreat from it all
  kiss it goodbye
oh sorrow
i still feel you
  somehow i must live that vibrant without
  the sweet apricot taste of rum

Ode to the child
I aborted
For I was sure
I would have more
Ode to the men
That left
For I knew
I would marry
Ode to the womb
That filled
And emptied
Earlier than most
For I thought
I would do it alone
Ode to a life
Of waiting
For I thought
Patience was a
Virtue and a
Form of reverence
To be rewarded
Later

TUESDAYS

Because I reached
And I stepped
And I fell

And I soared
And I bled
And I moved

All the while one stubborn red leaf danced before it died

Cry I said. Cry I did.
As my knees buckled
Onto the street and across the threshold
Into Meg's arms

We are three and half months
From your death
The leaf was green and then red and then today it is brown and
almost gone
A symbol that does not reflect my anguish
Which isn't dried up and still wonders if you will call

I miss you and don't seem to be willing to accept that you kept this
from me. That you were going to die and do it yourself – not tell
me.

So I say what I know
That I soar
And I bleed
And I leap and I fall

And one day
it moves

OF TIMES TRAVELLED

i.
I have spent
An abundance of time
Trying to understand
Why intelligence
In women
Is so frightening to men

For whatever it is
It makes me be

I have watched women
Become opaque
Slippery
Knowing that
Coquettish behavior
Is a means to a manipulation

For whatever it is
It makes me be

I get that I'm a cliche
Of scapegoating
Intense, passionate,
Holding many realities
At once
Before others

For whatever it is
It makes me be

I try to imagine
Saying less
And inevitably
Blurt out
All that nobody
Wants to hear

For whatever it is
It makes me be

I have imagined
Being that afraid
Choosing a man
Of limited intellect
But I knew
I would be so lonely

For whatever it is
It makes me be

So the choice is
Lonely alone
Or lonely with
And how many women
Feel this
Or are discounted for their
Substance

ii.
We all make our way
As best we can
Forced on journeys
We never chose

There is the
Undivinable course to life
Those things we must
Reconcile

If journeying is
Arduous
Undesired
Ambivalent

Then we must
Do all we can
To maintain hope
In that desert

And judgment
As an overlay
From peeking eyes
Becomes the burden
Intolerable

Know that no story
Is grasped
Maybe not even
From the inside

It is one
That curiosity
Should unfold
Like fresh linen
Spread for a dinner party

We miss these stories
Of the wise
The old and the plump
The utterly happy
And the hopeless

For I have lived them all
Not of my liking
There is so much
I have seen
And know

Which simple
Disregard
And assumption
Misses
Failing to relish in
Its richness

UNCLE CEREMONY

I held the mourning
for so long
close to me,
as if I was
clutching you
to my breast

I didn't want
to lose sight
of you – the
real sight –
and I knew

what everyone said
was true:
that time
healed all
wounds and
memories of you

would be gone.
And I needed you
your sage comfort
given with minimal
words. Un-flowery

but those
who could see
saw beyond the mirror
saw this man
standing in his
pinstripes to
my left

it was unfair
to keep you.
Still, for
a year
I refused to release
you from

your sense of duty
your desire to protect me
to watch over me
I cringed at
my selfishness
but still
I could not stop

finally, guilt
consumed me –
had you not given
me more than enough
peace?

Then
there was
ceremony
beautiful, grand
as stately as
you always were

and I put you to bed
sent you to wherever
you could go.
That singed my edges –
as I felt the absence
of you as my cloak

a protection
and presence you
had always quietly
gifted to me
even when I was
too young to recognize it

mom asks,
"do you miss him?"
to which I respond,
"all the time, every day"
and I clutch my chest
where you live
as a small blister of
longing and appreciation

YOU KNOW THINGS

you know things
You
know things
You *know* things

you've been down this
road before
you know what
it means
to engage people with trauma
who haven't had therapy

who mean well
but cannot
who don't have Ifá
who make you feel sick

maybe
maybe I will
go back to my cave
to my knowing things
to my place of forfeiture

the place where
i don't have to ask
a million insecure
questions
where feeling unsettled
is clearly you
not me

boxed into secret
hopes and years
of prince charming
beliefs or
that at some point we
all get it right
i forge toward freckles
and lost nights of sleep
that roll toward uncertainty

this poem is not
done
but
in the middle
the middle of something utterly unknown
leaving me untethered
still stitching
into this tapestry

don't bother
Don't bother
don't bother to come here
and try to explain
for i already know
i already do
and all i need
is for you to answer
are you ambivalent
about me?
and can you even do it
if you're not?

you know things
You
know things

you know things
about yourself
that i do not
i need information
and choice
and not to be a hostaged beard
or a fool
or a chump
holding my heart
in my palm
like a beggar's cup

SAD SONG FOR A NATION
(December 2016)

It is a sad day when you lose
That which you have fought for in
Your marrow, your bones

Lost to greed
Lost to lies
Lost to jokes

> *I have hunter green phlegm*
> *What does that mean?*
> *It ran away from itself*
> *Because it was so utterly obscene*

What did the earth say on that day?
We know through the equation of elements
Science by definition is only factual
It cannot lie
Theorems that lead to truth
It's called an "exact science."

> *In Chinese medicine*
> *Lungs represent grief*
> *And I can't catch my breath*

In the genesis
Amidst death and bloodshed
Founding fathers knew
The predictable nature of man
To fear and control and dominate.

These elements, constitutional elements
Are here for a reason
And like your faith
It is so easy to use it to manage
A fear of not getting enough
Using spirit to be cruel
Not trusting you will be taken care of –

I took too much Mucinex DM today
we had to call poison control
I threw up hot lava and it was
Dry and chemical and pulled at every inch of my tissues

Everywhere I go
I hear people hacking
We are a Nation in loss

I had a thought about death
in the midst of the floating
violence
it's been hard for me here and I thought
leaving would be ok

And then you remember
God sees all
And the birds are still singing
Joyous at the absolute
Hour of survival

Ever the resilience of spirit
That is man
Is that denial or perpetuity?
Even still, we go on.

But then I thought no
I still believe some things are
Possible for me
I still have hope that
There will be change and love and kindness

It is that appreciation
That allows us to love others
To see people individually
I know
God's time not mine
Unfortunately. My heart needs to heal from this disappointment
And the healing requires we purge him from its very tissue and
that is painful.

I want back the foundation
Of democracy
The one we tried to uphold
And failed
But was the backbone
Of our safety
Because knowing it is there
Prevents chaos, creates aspiration and striving.

I'm the idea that all men
Are created equal
That each person with their
Own fears, and marrow, and reactions,
And sinewy tissue
Is a miracle of being that engenders
Awe and dignity

And we can believe again.

ZIGGY

Something precious came to me
~~And~~ it was a moment of hating you
After months of wanting to slit my wrists and hunt you
down
Peace came in my disdain

You with your arrogance
And judgment
You never even noticed how tolerant I was
When you told me you never
"Got David Bowie"
That you didn't think he was
"That talented"
Which you said with all the arrogance of a conga player
With a 13" drum

I was so tired though
Tired from pain
Tired from the war
That ensued by dating you
Which was directed solely at me
I saw your idiocy
And didn't point it out
I let you run wild
Like a banshee
In all the ways that women are supposedly

Off

And later
When you left ~~me~~
You accused me of so many things:

Needing ~~always~~ to be right
Being judgmental
Believing in leprechauns
Being kooky

Yet <u>you</u> wore
The Mardi Gras dress
And patchwork quilt pants ~~Charlie Bucket~~
And feared I only had "pathetic sex"
Because I loved you more than your sartorial choices
~~clown shoes~~

And you never understood
The intergalactic rock star
Shaman
Who was always ~~going to be~~
Kinder than you

MONTERA

friends from junior high
found me
yesterday,
I was pleased
they're all so kind
Susannah asked,
"did you tell them anything
about yourself?"
– reminding me I live outside the box –
"what?"
"well, that you're sober thirty-five years,
that you've had this intensely shamanic path?"
"yeah," I said, "I lead with
'I see dead people' –
that always goes over well"

I want and need friends
friends that aren't about all this
whatever happened to me
I am still myself
"you must survive"
is a mantra we hold
without knowing that until we must
whatever happened
makes sense somewhere
other than here

CHATTANOOGA

(Who do you do
And how do you fais do-do)

I am a poet
A New Yorker
An Òrìsà person

So you can see I admire
Your lyric

I am a truth teller
A vision seeker

I am high on the words that you wrote
And low on the current humanity

I know that   *Mumbo Jumbo*
I took it down from

West 9th Street NYC
Flew to Market and found

I had traversed some of the same ground
You just half a block away

As I trip the light fantastic
Down this corner

Pass your curtains billow
All great forms arrive there
I imagine because I have never
Been star struck but   with a mind?
A mind staring up at the same moon

Shining down through the smell of camel and subway turnstiles
and then
eucalyptus dew

Did you ride that night
Train through the desert
To Maydoom to find your secret jangle?

Or was it Harlem post renaissance
That brought you down to the funktastic
Vodou crawl of an anti-discipline flaming word spitter?
No mind, I don't care

Four score and
This world is a whore
all bound up and afraid of an intelligent
Black man with his sensuality
on the outside, you said no
Brought it all out   carved
The way for so many who didn't even
Know they needed to see or say or call or
Summon into being

The voice of the Lwa and the
Rulers of marketplace
And those witches that sit in
That Magnolia tree down
From your house

Speak. Speak for those that
Are afraid and have been beaten
Speak. Speak for those of us
Wild in monotheism and Africa
Speak. Speak for that of the ethereal

Spoken.

LEPIDOPTERA

I do not long for you anymore
(For I realize you are not it)
Not what I never got
From my father or any other man
Not someone who could stay still
In the face of emotion that urges us intensely into flight
Not someone I have yearned for who is like me
(Who has done the peering into the depths that I have/who will
allow themselves to be rocked/with the swaying of the ship of core
pain/and the tremors of the earthquake of core panic/but still
refuse to injure/for some hope and faith/some desire of grace/
carried you through to the other side/where there might be
another like you).

I remember watching a giant moth in the bush
Hang on the flashbulb of the cameraman
Near six inches at its' wingspan
Surrounded by so many other bugs
Beautiful yellow and velvety cream
Lined the ribcage as it danced above me almost unmoving
Ever hopeful of some vision
And wish for abundance and

I thought,

That is what those who trudge the internal path are doing
Traveling into the night
In the dense bush.
Risking green mambas and killer ants.
Through mosquitos that buzz the dewy air around them.
Searching deeper and deeper for this inland light.
Of grace. And the true bone and blood

Of fellow travelers.

AS THE BOW BREAKS, PART FOUR

My heart is broken
You
Are an old man now
We
finally have
Six years of peace between us
It is lovely and quiet
You're still overwhelmed by
My intensity
And
I still recoil at your
Intransigence but
You are softer
Humbled by age
By your feet that stumble
By your head that shakes

We sit
Over Indian food
At the Travelodge and
There is a sadness about this
Your end
My health problems
Your shrinking independence
I dare not cry
Because it isn't about me
But it is always there
Welled to the point of
A croak in my heart and
I'm lost in trying to enjoy
the times we never had before and
Knowing they aren't enough

We were robbed by all the fences
That needed mending
By Parkinson's and Lyme and Cancer
By your devotion to your new
second wife who you
married at seventy
Who marries at seventy?
Oh yes, you do
And I come back to the man
Who raised me
Who taught me how to work
And think
And be devotional to
Something and many things
Who understood shamanism
And my spiritual path
More than my emotional
Pain

The bubble containing my heart
Begins to fill and crack so
I lash it back with a whip fiercely
And we order your favorite
Baingan Bharta
And slip into
Our familiar talk
Of politics

A SEA OF KISSES

One kiss to
Make me stay
Two to
Start the day
Three and
I'm on my way

DAWN

I have never been
　　The one
　　　　That got away
　　　　　　All bogged down
　　　　　　　　With illnesses
　　　　　　　　　　And ghosts
　　　　　　　　　　　　And Òrìsà born taboos
I am born of
　　The reluctant cloth
　　　　Governess of the harsh
I spin into realities
　　Battles that
　　　　I endure
　　　　　　Tread
　　　　　　　　My way to the top
　　　　　　　　　　Holding breath
　　　　　　　　　　　　Through the great
　　　　　　　　　　　　　　Suffering of waves
　　　　　　　　　　　　　　　　Thrashing about
　　　　　　　　　　　　　　　　　　Disoriented
Cherishing the
　　Mundane of a
　　　　Moment of a
　　　　　　Smile or a
　　　　　　　　Kindness
And if I need to flee
　　I can't think of why
　　　　For as the beaded Prince once said,
　　　　　　"There is reason for everything"
So the weight of
　　Sodden sloshing
　　　　In the wet woolens of

My work and my world
        Means I am running nowhere
        Fast
            And probably reflect a
                Frozen experience of
                Difficulty
But within this
    I cherish
        The hummingbird that
            Sits with me
                At Ògún
        The sun that
            Breaks through the fog
                At Egbé
        The crows that
            Call me
                To Èsù and Ifa
        The honeyed sound of
                The bell of Òsun
And I am glad for my
    Magical baggage
        And purity of purpose

YOU WILL HAVE TO EAT PIZZA WITH YOUR FRIENDS

I told you last night
In the kitchen
And realized   Finally
That you do love me

"Why?" you asked and said
I was "fine with it for months"

"It's a building effect   the yeast and sugar"
"Sugar creates fungus?"
          A sad "yes" echoed out my mouth from the pantry
"And you're heartier than me" I said as I wondered about
my Berber tribe, likely inbred, too many flies on meats and a
weak immune system

But still you come here
          To eat with me
My body misshapen
By so many betrayals
Offers no promise of erotic elevation

And yet, here you sit,
In chairs too small
That hurt your back
Eating "weird" food

Because you see the long goal of love
          The promise of connection
The knowledge that I worship
A different God
But one who still counts on me
To be better than most

Maybe I'm sad about the pizza because I
know
That like the building of yeast
Even the long goal of love and its' deep promise
Can't overwhelm the idiosyncrasies of my life. Which are
greater than many
And I don't want to lose you
Yet another loss to the choice
made for me   The one by the Irúnmolè
For me to sit close and
Listen
Listen
Listen
For next words and direction

Pizza now the simple-ness
Of love and digestion
Something easier

SCHLAN

Sometimes when I am blind
I think of all the right things to say
And when there is a drought
I no longer want rain

When we do this every year about the rainfall I think this is like
the famous *Who's on First*. It is our shtick. We have many. You're so
serious about it. And I'm so irritated that you won't admit there is
enough snowpack. "There were avalanches in Tahoe" I yell out.
But I'm always forgetting what it was like when I thought I would
lose you. When you lay there with a tube up your throat and out
your nose. And choked on your saliva. And more than that.

I can't do this without you. Never been able to. I can't say that all
the time or I'd be crying all day. But maybe now, you are not in a
drought. And you have just enough water in your cells to make it
through more days. And I want to celebrate that with you.

TARRYTOWN

Tarrytown to Pendleton to Phoenix
Turn left at the Big Rock
Jump back
From the Great Highway
To the Bison Notch
Some time before the land
Is gone
Before the whales
Are all ashore

More grey whales in the Bay
Searching for food
died
Hit by ships
And yet,
Here on these lands
I made an offering to the dead
And someone asked me a question
Which was really a statement
That saccharine voice oh so angry
"Why are you leaving things all over the neighborhood"
Why do you think you own the place?
Certainly self considered
"Woke"
With a BLM sign on her lawn
Didn't talk about me on Next Door
Or call the police-so that's good-I didn't die
But it is its own insult
As Middle-Aged White Women
Get all the shit as it rolls down hill
Even from their own kind
And she was up in my grill

Standing in my chancletas and Ilekes
I missed NY's
head-down-don't-fuck-with-it form of social control
We have religious freedom in this country
But in the name of tolerance
Nobody tolerates anyone

This land is not big enough for all of us
With the heat rising and the need
To be six thousand feet away from anyone
Who doesn't
Perfectly bend to your narcissistic needs
Because that's what this is

And

Do the koalas care that we rip each other apart here with cancel
culture or if I feed the dead on my corners or do they just want us
to stop scorching the earth

UNTITLED TILDA SWINTON POEM

It was one of those strange hot NY summer Sundays. August. Late afternoon. The city was quiet. A summer reality I still love. Minus the 94 degrees and baking with a hot soot filled breeze blowing at me, pelting grit into my eyes. I crossed the north side of 23rd street through the intersection of 3rd avenue heading towards Lex. I was the only person on the block.

I looked across the street and on the south side, I saw them. Tilda and her striking young man. And maybe it was because this was before Madison Park frou frou-ness had been invented - and before the Rose Bar and all the pretension that would ensue - that I was the only one there. She was grace and androgyny and a female juxtaposition of my great love Bowie. They meandered and danced off each other pulled to and from one another by the laziness of heat and the electricity of their erotic flirtation. She had long golden flowing things and I stumbled weighted with the plastic bags of groceries that pulled at my NY life's arms. Stopping every few minutes to rest on the sidewalk and pump, bringing blood back into them. I had done this movement hundreds of thousands of times, and still wondered if I was really going to commit myself to a life of the Grocery Bag Flexion. They played forward and backward stealing touches and kisses in a gentle Merce Cunningham way.

I was invisible. Dripping in sweat while they looked fixed in powder. Enjoying the privacy of my moment - my limited life uplifted by witnessing someone I knew to be all counterpart and passion and mind. My mind hidden behind a sopping wet t-shirt and 7 days worth of cayenne and lemons. They weren't even dirty. They could have been floating on the Mediterranean Sea. And then, they did. We reached the opposite corners and parted. Them without knowing me - I had no unique dance to offer. Me clomping off with overstretched limbs to my dumpy apartment. Grateful to have stolen this secret moment of magical mundane. Few heroes are so substantial and punk rock and themselves.

AFTER THE FALL—A LOVE SONG

There is music playing
Everywhere you stand
A celebration of your life
All those you helped and taught and healed

After the fall
You lost your ability to conduct with your hands
Lost your ability to travel the rough terrain
Of the higher notes

Over mountains
Through time zones
Alone
To where the whippoorwill
Lulled you

You with your camera's eye and silent verse

After the fall
All I thought about was your death
And that every moment could be
Our last
I'm not getting enough time

I don't want to be here
Without you
And that is the song I sing
Not the happy call of the whippoorwill
But the lone cry of the loon on Dog Cove
Left alone in the beginning of fall
Too heavy to take flight yet with low winds

After the fall
You knew it too
You knew your life had changed forever
Notes you wrote in your orchestration, quietly
The angry crescendo over such helplessness
You never shared

I could have tolerated
The persistent trill of the bohemian waxwing
I'm scared. I'm lonely. I'm excited to see you.
All the notes sung mostly in Canada and occasionally New England.
You left those calls in another country.

After the fall
Your story still grew as you
Refined the place that gave you care
Humbly sounding your signature drum
Taught that the pride of life is the notes that linger
Not the ones with your name

But on this day
I call you out father
I sing out my love song for the man
Who taught me to persevere with my betraying human form
And allow the mourning dove to both
Soothe and unearth the grief in others

After the fall
The unspoken song
Means the most.

AND ONE DAY YOU WILL DANCE

And one day you will dance
Down within the Mayfair to and fro
Under the heavens
That's the way things go

And one day you will dance

You've lived in shadows
But the night sky will brighten
Ever alight with the possibility of the living
Pushing yourself from one end of the street to the other—this long
race adding traction within the decline

And one day you will dance

Because God finally saw fit to give you peace

Peace from all the relics of yesterday who roam the earth speaking
to the shaman banished in a corner—outside the realm that doesn't
commune with spirits
Merely influenced by them

Peace from all the disappointments of human frailty and judgment
The stars will bob on each stone
walkway to hope
like garden lights to a party
One in which you are not outside the group looking in and people
don't always ask you to accept that they can't accept you

And one day you will dance

As fifty comes and goes and you accept a different life's purpose and hold onto every hand you touched and the ripple of the stone's throw that skimmed the water
Because who said actions make the man
And you said we would dance together and now you're not here

And one day I will dance

Dance the joy of the simple things that arrived at my door and that death left me be and allowed me to hear a thousand birds
Maybe not for love but for surviving as a seer on that quantum razors edge and still helping to make things better

That day is today.

OH SPACE

Shoot south. Not north. Because it's all going downhill fast. As you celebrate your bills with a rocket of delight and those below dream of the same chance instead of holding you to some sort of appropriate stance. The news is bad. All bad. Did they do it? Shift us to no rights while we celebrated their climb?

WOLVES

Today, I watched an old friend die
But as I did, I remembered his poetic gaze
Thought of the loss of his mind
Knew he would have called a moratorium
On debating
And spoken beautifully
For the chosen

"Silence the headlines!"
"Still the hands!"
"Bring back countenance!"
For the love we have lost

Nobody ring the noon bell
There is no victory here
Whilst mourning doves sing
We have lost those that
Carry the wisdom of such
Social graces

"Climb high" he told me
At my publishing rejections
Filling the dark corners of every stage
Insisting we
"Maintain an appreciation for art about love and death"
But today, told me I would have to go that alone

And so I ask for a minute
A minute away from the chatter
As I light a candle
Place him on the altar of my dead
Allow him to drink and smoke in the afterlife

He would have appreciated that
As I elevate him

Something done. For we hear no words for the dead, no Kaddish spoken, no holy sacrament, no presidential singing of "Amazing Grace," not a word to the earth making this less abstract, not a hand held or tear shed. Not a simple goodbye.

I hold the sacred minute for you, my friend. I'll sing the birdsong of your life. I'll dust back the stages that won't be the same with your loss. I'll spill the ink and tip the paint. Strike the set I say. I will hold reverence for you.

QUEBRAR HACHA

Step
To me with more than
I owe you nothing
And conspiracy theories

For I remember the boy
Horizontal across my bed
Like timber fell
Something like Hickory

Eyes up at me
A glint in Tuscarora blue moons
Who lifted one hand
And cradled my cheekbone

Trusting me with pins
Inserted for a headache
The steeliness we have now
Remote

Not even in the shadows

MOTHER

And god came into your soul
And said,
"You will rise from the legacy
Of your mother's sickness
And your father's philandering
Giving you a child's spirit
And in that joy you will participate in the gifts of the earth
You will teach your daughters that way!"

That way:
you
bound through the forest
you
quiet yourself with the hollow call of the loon

Not of makeup and tampons
But of mind and essence
Gifts that carry us through the darkest hours

You are with me always my mother
You say it's always being there – the being a "mummy"
At 82 still stunning, putting up Christmas trees. Skiing all the days
you can.

I wish I'd given you the joy of a grandchild
You could've taught them
How to listen to your heart internally
as you struggle up Chocorua
How to keep going
when you're not sure it will ever stop
How to cherish the rose you left for me
when you went back home

It was pressed. Pressed and conflated like the picture of memories you gave me. All sounds and smells and snap of a twig on a bed of pine needles. Those things that become the tonal image of one's being. The flavor of the interior. Of a person. That is communicated into all things done future present and past. The existent sound of your boots behind me encouraging me up Rattlesnake when I was so small my legs wobbled in placement. The grace of your soul imparted from yours to mine.

ACKNOWLEDGMENTS

First to Olódùmarè and all the Irúnmolè who have saved my life and been my deepest relationships. To my Egungun who have stood by my side. To my Ori and Òsun who guided me. To the countless Babaláwo and Ìyánífá of Nigeria and Cuba who taught me Ifá over decades and confirmed the importance of Ìwà Pèlé. To Sarah Lawrence for teaching me how to write and think independently. The single best educational experience of my life. To my father for teaching me resilience and the value of Ela. To my mother who taught me how to appreciate nature and people with Ìwà Rere. To my sister who has been my best friend and interminable supporter ever since we were kids playing in secret at 2am. To my friends everywhere who loved me in spite of feeling helpless; some more determined to save me and others determined to make me laugh through it. To my clients for trusting me to walk them through the dark night of the soul ever inspiring my admiration. To MJ who through the cloud of an 8 ball and ridiculous arrogance, inspired one of my favorite poems in this book. To TG, you can eat pizza here any time.

ABOUT THE AUTHOR

Lauren Martin is a psychotherapist, poet, and devoted
Ìyânífá. She studied poetry at Sarah Lawrence College.
She spent years writing without submitting her work
due to a long shamanic journey that led her to both
Ifá and the writing of this collection of poems. Lauren
lives in Oakland, California.

SELECTED TITLES FROM SHE WRITES PRESS

She Writes Press is an independent publishing company founded to serve women writers everywhere. Visit us at www.shewritespress.com.

Benediction for a Black Swan by Mimi Zollars. $14.95, 978-1-63152-950-4. A lush, provocative collection of poems about childhood, children, marriage, divorce, alcoholism, and the sensual world.

The Lucidity Project by Abbey Campbell Cook. $16.95, 978-1-63152-032-7. After suffering from depression all her life, twenty-five-year-old Max Dorigan joins a mysterious research project on a Caribbean island, where she's introduced to the magical and healing world of lucid dreaming.

Trespassers by Andrea Miles. $16.95, 978-1-63152-903-0. Sexual abuse survivor Melanie must make a choice: choose forgiveness and begin to heal from her emotional wounds, or exact revenge for the crimes committed against her—even if it destroys her family.

Moon Water by Pam Webber. $16.95, 978-1-63152-675-6. Nettie, a gritty sixteen-year-old, is already reeling from a series of sucker punches when an old medicine woman for the Monacan Indians gives her a cryptic message about a coming darkness: a blood moon whose veiled danger threatens Nettie and those she loves. To survive, Nettie and her best friend, Win, will have to scour the perilous mountains for Nature's ancient but perfect elements and build a mysterious dreamcatcher.

Beginning with Cannonballs by Jill McCroskey Coupe. $16.95, 978-1-63152-848-4. In segregated Knoxville, Tennessee, Hanna (black) and Gail (white) share a crib as infants and remain close friends into their teenage years—but as they grow older, careers, marriage, and a tragic death further strain their already complicated friendship.

South of Everything by Audrey Taylor Gonzalez. $16.95, 978-1-63152-949-8. A powerful parable about the changing South after World War II, told through the eyes of young white woman whose friendship with her parents' black servant, Old Thomas, initiates her into a world of magic and spiritual richness.